D0920087

Joy Journal:

Make Joy a Daily Experience

Rebecca Kochenderfer

Copyright © 2013 by Rebecca Kochenderfer
All rights reserved.

Published in the United States of America

Homeschool.com, Inc.
12210 Herdal Drive, Suite 11
Auburn, CA
95603
Editor@Homeschool.com

ISBN: 978-0-9816171-1-4
1. Self-Improvement 2. Journals 3. Spirituality

Cover Design and Layout by Spring Moon

"My days are fun, productive, and filled with delightful surprises."

Introduction

Most likely, your life is already pretty wonderful. But sometimes life gets busy and we forget how much we have to be grateful for.

Joy Journal helps you to remember all the little things in your life that bring you joy. It prompts you to decide ahead of time the type of wonderful day you are going to have. It helps you to appreciate your current life more, and gently leads you to new habits and new ways of thinking that can make your life even better.

Week 1 "What Brings You Joy?"

Week 2 "Say Yes More Often"

Week 3 "My Days are Fun, Productive and Filled With Delightful Surprises"

Week 4 "Keystone Habits"

Week 5 "Focus on What You Want, Not On What You Don't Want"

Week 6 "The Universe is Just Throwing Money at Me!"

Week 7 "Self-Fulfilling Prophecy"

Week 8 "Act As If..."

Week 9 "The Power of Visualization"

Week 10 "Set Yourself Up For Success"

Week 11 "What Are You Excited About?"

Week 12 "Taking Care of Yourself"

Joy Journal takes you on a journey of self-discovery. This is your chance to re-discover joy and to make joy a daily experience.

Wishing you a journey of joyful discovery,

Rebecca Kochenderfer

Week 1

"What Brings You Joy?"

Here's an experiment you can try that I call, "The Joy Experiment." For one week, decide that you are only going to do things that you enjoy. No have-to's or should do's. This is a week for want-to's.

I tried this experiment for a week and I was surprised by the results.

On Day 1, my happiness and joy came from watching TV and eating pizza (basically, from resting).

On Day 2, my happiness came from walking 8 miles and by being productive.

Day 3, was not a joyful day, no matter how much I wanted it to be. There was something I really wanted that I didn't get. I didn't know it at the time, but there was a reason I wasn't supposed to get that thing. There was something I needed to learn by not getting it.

The week progressed and joy took on a different form each day. If I had stopped the experiment after Day 1, I would have thought that the key to joy was rest and pizza. But each day was different.

Sometimes joy came from resting, sometimes from keeping busy. Sometimes from being alone, and sometimes by being around others.

When I started out the week, my goal was to feel joyful every minute of every day. But I discovered that, at least for me, joy is not possible or even desirable every minute of every day. Sometimes there is a bigger purpose at work.

If you have a chance to do the full Joy Experiment, I recommend it. Starting now, promise yourself that this week you are not going to do anything you don't "want" to do.

You may think you don't want to go to work, but you will probably discover that you do want to go because you want that paycheck. You may decide that you don't "want" to do the dishes, but in the end you either do them because you want to have things clean, or you don't do them and no harm comes from it. Contrary to popular belief, the earth will not open up and swallow you if you do what you want to do, instead of what you have to do.

This week you are going to discover the things that bring you joy. This is no small thing. Joy is unique to each person and is often elusive. We get so wrapped up in the busy-ness of our days that we forget how beautiful and fleeting life is.

Joy Journal focuses your attention so that it's easier for you to tune into the joy that is already all around you.

Monday

To-Do's

Week 1 - "What Brings You Joy?"

Monday

What joyful things are you looking forward to today?

_____

_____

_____

What brought you joy today?

_____

_____

_____

Did you experience any "joy killers" today?

_____

_____

_____

_____

What are you grateful for today?

_____

_____

_____

_____

Tuesday

Tuesday

What joyful things are you looking forward to today?

_____

_____

_____

_____

What brought you joy today?

_____

_____

_____

_____

Did you experience any "joy killers" today?

_____

_____

_____

_____

What are you grateful for today?

_____

_____

_____

_____

Wednesday

Wednesday

What joyful things are you looking forward to today?

_____

_____

_____

_____

What brought you joy today?

_____

_____

_____

_____

Did you experience any "joy killers" today?

_____

_____

_____

_____

What are you grateful for today?

_____

_____

_____

_____

Thursday

Thursday

What joyful things are you looking forward to today?

_____

_____

_____

_____

What brought you joy today?

_____

_____

_____

Did you experience any "joy killers" today?

_____

_____

_____

What are you grateful for today?

_____

_____

_____

_____

Friday

To-Do's

Friday

What joyful things are you looking forward to today?

_____

_____

_____

_____

What brought you joy today?

_____

_____

_____

Did you experience any "joy killers" today?

_____

_____

_____

What are you grateful for today?

_____

_____

_____

_____

Saturday & Sunday

Today is a day for freedom.
Not a day for have-to's or should-do's.
It's a day for want-to's.

Today is a day of exploration.
Armed only with a journal, a pen and a cup of tea,
You set off on a journey of self-discovery.

Today is a day for asking for what you want.
Table inside too noisy? Politely ask to move to the patio and voila! you are there.
Why don't we ask for what we want more often?

Today is a day for choices.
Will you go to the gym? Maybe, maybe not.
Reading out on the deck? Absolutely.

Today you are the leading role, the above-the-title player.
Not your partner, not the kids.
You are the heroine, the protagonist, the leading lady in your life.

What did you discover this week about your have-to's, should-do's, and want-to's?

_____

_____

_____

_____

_____

_____

What did you discover about joy?

_____

_____

_____

_____

_____

_____

Are there any changes you want to make in your life, based on what you learned this week?

_____

_____

_____

_____

_____

_____

Week 2

"Say 'Yes' More Often"

In Jim Carey's movie, "Yes Man," the main character has a life-changing experience when, for one week, he decides to say "yes" to every opportunity that is presented to him. I thought that was a great idea so I decided to give it a try. For one week, I said "yes" to everything. "Can you join us for a movie?" Yes. "Want to come to my daughter's concert?" Yes. "You really should replace your old phone with an iPhone. I think you'll love it." Yes.

I discovered a lot about myself that week. I discovered that I say "no" a lot. Oftentimes my knee-jerk response is, "No thanks. I don't have the time, the money, the energy." Yet when I did say "yes" to everything, I felt great. I did have the time, the energy and the money. And it was so much fun!

This week, I invite you to play "The Yes Game." The mini version of this game is to just turn the page and follow this week's journal prompts. This will give you some great insights into where you say "yes" and where you say "no" in your life.

If you have the time and the courage to play the full version of "The Yes Game," it will reveal things about you that will surprise you. One woman discovered that no one ever asks her for anything because she has a history of always taking charge and of being super independent.

If you play the full version of The Yes Game, I encourage you to try it for a full week, and I caution you not to tell anyone what you are doing. That way you will get honest results and you won't have to worry about anyone taking advantage of you.

What will you discover when you play The Yes Game? Will you find out that you have a lack mentality when it comes to time or money? Will you discover that you have a hard time saying "no" to people? **Will you uncover hidden dreams that you want to say "yes" to?** Here's to your week of "yes" and to more yeses in life.

Monday

Monday

What are you going to say "yes" to today?

_____
_____
_____
_____

How did "yes" show up in your life today?

_____
_____
_____
_____

Was there anything you said "no" to, or wanted to say "no" to? What were your reasons?

_____
_____
_____

What are you grateful for today?

_____
_____
_____
_____

Tuesday

Tuesday

What are you going to say "yes" to today?

_____

_____

_____

_____

How did "yes" show up in your life today?

_____

_____

_____

_____

Was there anything you said "no" to, or wanted to say "no" to? What were your reasons?

_____

_____

_____

What are you grateful for today?

_____

_____

_____

_____

Wednesday

Wednesday

What are you going to say "yes" to today?

_____

_____

_____

_____

How did "yes" show up in your life today?

_____

_____

_____

Was there anything you said "no" to, or wanted to say "no" to? What were your reasons?

_____

_____

_____

What are you grateful for today?

_____

_____

_____

_____

Thursday

Thursday

What are you going to say "yes" to today?

_____

_____

_____

_____

How did "yes" show up in your life today?

_____

_____

_____

_____

Was there anything you said "no" to, or wanted to say "no" to?
What were your reasons?

_____

_____

_____

What are you grateful for today?

_____

_____

_____

_____

_____

Friday

To-Do's

Friday

What are you going to say "yes" to today?

_____

_____

_____

_____

How did "yes" show up in your life today?

_____

_____

_____

_____

Was there anything you said "no" to, or wanted to say "no" to?
What were your reasons?

_____

_____

_____

What are you grateful for today?

_____

_____

_____

_____

Saturday & Sunday

What did you learn from your experiences this week?

_____

_____

_____

_____

_____

_____

_____

_____

_____

_____

Are there things you want to start saying "yes" to?

Are there things you want to start saying "no" to?

Week 3

"My Days are Fun, Productive, and Filled with Delightful Surprises"

Quantum Physicists have discovered that when they look at the smallest particles known to man, the mere fact that they are observing these particles changes how these particles act. This caused one scientist to wonder if he could pre-determine how his day was going to turn out. So from that day forward, this scientist decided that every day he would take a moment to write out a brief description of the kind of day he wanted to have that day.

I invite you to do the same. This week, decide ahead of time that your days are going to be fun, productive and filled with delightful surprises.

Delightful surprises can be big or little. One time I asked for a big surprise. I asked for divine confirmation that I was "not alone, that I was loved, and that I was being guarded and guided." I received an out-of-the-blue call from my daughter saying, "Mom, I just had the weirdest experience and had to tell you about it." Someone had come up to her and used almost the exact words I had asked for. It gave me goose bumps.

But most days my delightful surprises come in little, unexpected ways, like a deer in the front yard, or a rainbow, or a hummingbird at my window. **What will your surprises be?**

Monday

To-Do's

Week 3 - "My Days Are Fun, Productive and Filled With Delightful Surprises"

Monday

What are you going to do that is fun today?

_____

_____

How will you be productive today?

_____

_____

Did your day go as planned? Why or why not?

_____

_____

_____

Did you experience any delightful surprises today?

_____

_____

_____

What are you grateful for today?

_____

_____

_____

_____

Tuesday

Tuesday

What are you going to do that is fun today?

_____

_____

How will you be productive today?

_____

_____

Did your day go as planned? Why or why not?

_____

_____

_____

Did you experience any delightful surprises today?

_____

_____

_____

What are you grateful for today?

_____

_____

_____

_____

Wednesday

Wednesday

What are you going to do that is fun today?

_____

_____

How will you be productive today?

_____

_____

Did your day go as planned? Why or why not?

_____

_____

_____

Did you experience any delightful surprises today?

_____

_____

_____

What are you grateful for today?

_____

_____

_____

_____

Thursday

Thursday

What are you going to do that is fun today?

_____

_____

How will you be productive today?

_____

_____

Did your day go as planned? Why or why not?

_____

_____

_____

Did you experience any delightful surprises today?

_____

_____

_____

What are you grateful for today?

_____

_____

_____

_____

Friday

To-Do's

Week 3 - "My Days Are Fun, Productive and Filled With Delightful Surprises"

Friday

What are you going to do that is fun today?

_____

_____

How will you be productive today?

_____

_____

Did your day go as planned? Why or why not?

_____

_____

_____

Did you experience any delightful surprises today?

_____

_____

_____

What are you grateful for today?

_____

_____

_____

_____

Saturday & Sunday

Did the sentence: "My days are fun, productive and filled with delightful surprises" work for you? If not, is there another sentence that would work better for you? What would that be?

_____

_____

_____

_____

_____

_____

_____

_____

_____

_____

What did you learn about "delightful surprises?"

_____

_____

_____

_____

_____

_____

_____

Was it helpful for you to pre-plan your day? In general, did your days go as you planned?

_____

_____

_____

_____

_____

_____

_____

Did you find that having positive expectations for your day helped you to have a better day?

_____

_____

_____

_____

_____

_____

_____

Week 4

"Keystone Habits"

Research shows that 40% of our actions each day are habitual. We do the same things every day, day after day, out of habit. Our habits drive us and they can either help us or hold us back.

Some habits, called keystone habits, are particularly powerful. A keystone habit is a habit that leads you to other habits, either good or bad. For example, exercising tends to be a positive keystone habit. Once you develop the exercise habit, it leads to other positive habits, like eating healthier. For some people, quitting smoking is a positive keystone habit that leads to exercising and eating healthier. An example of a negative keystone habit is eating sweets for breakfast. For many people, this leads to poor eating habits throughout the day.

Keystone habits are powerful because you only have to pick one positive habit to work on and other, related habits, just fall into place.

This week you are going to choose a new habit that you want to develop – a good keystone habit that you believe will lead you to other good habits.

One of the best ways to develop habits is to use a "trigger" to remind you to do that habit. For example:

* If you put your vitamins out on the counter, instead of tucked away in a cupboard, this may act as a trigger to get you to take your vitamins. Taking your vitamins then becomes a positive keystone habit, because it leads you to other positive habits like eating fruits and vegetables or exercising or drinking more water.

* If you put your yoga mat or your running shoes or your workout clothes by your bedroom door, this may trigger you to exercise. And then, because you feel so virtuous about exercising, you develop other good habits, like being more active or eating healthier or getting to bed earlier.

Not all keystone habits are positive. This week, you may discover that you have developed some less than desirable keystone habits too. For example:

* You may discover that you have a habit of starting your day by eating Coco Puffs, and that this negative keystone habit leads you to habitually eating sweets the rest of the day.

* You may find that you have a habit of watching TV in the morning and that this habit is a negative keystone habit because it is leading you to other negative habits, like being less active, not exercising, eating potato chips, not cleaning the house, or not looking for the job you want.

Everyone is different. A habit that may be a negative keystone habit for one person can be a positive keystone habit for another person. Hot chocolate, for example, may trigger junk food eating in one person. But it may trigger relaxation for you, which leads you to a stress-free day.

Just play with it this week. Follow the journal prompts and see what comes up for you. In the Weekend Wrap-up section, **you can make some choices about which habits you want to keep and which you want to change**. Don't be hard on yourself. Treat it like a game and have fun with it.

Monday

To-Do's

Monday

What positive keystone habit will you experiment with today?

_____

_____

_____

Did that keystone habit lead you to other positive habits?

_____

_____

_____

Did you notice any habits you did today that you would like to keep?

_____

_____

_____

Did you find yourself doing any bad habits today that you would like to change?

_____

_____

_____

What are you grateful for today?

_____

_____

_____

Tuesday

To-Do's

Tuesday

What positive keystone habit will you experiment with today?

_____

_____

_____

Did that keystone habit lead you to other positive habits?

_____

_____

_____

Did you notice any habits you did today that you would like to keep?

_____

_____

_____

Did you find yourself doing any bad habits today that you would like to change?

_____

_____

_____

What are you grateful for today?

_____

_____

_____

Wednesday

Wednesday

What positive keystone habit will you experiment with today?

_____

_____

_____

Did that keystone habit lead you to other positive habits?

_____

_____

_____

Did you notice any habits you did today that you would like to keep?

_____

_____

_____

Did you find yourself doing any bad habits today that you would like to change?

_____

_____

_____

What are you grateful for today?

_____

_____

_____

Thursday

Thursday

What positive keystone habit will you experiment with today?

_____

_____

_____

Did that keystone habit lead you to other positive habits?

_____

_____

_____

Did you notice any habits you did today that you would like to keep?

_____

_____

_____

Did you find yourself doing any bad habits today that you would like to change?

_____

_____

_____

What are you grateful for today?

_____

_____

_____

Friday

Friday

What positive keystone habit will you experiment with today?

_____

_____

_____

Did that keystone habit lead you to other positive habits?

_____

_____

_____

Did you notice any habits you did today that you would like to keep?

_____

_____

_____

Did you find yourself doing any bad habits today that you would like to change?

_____

_____

_____

What are you grateful for today?

_____

_____

_____

Saturday & Sunday

Now that you've experimented with different keystone habits this week, did you find one habit in particular that you think will be very powerful for you?

_____

_____

_____

_____

_____

_____

_____

_____

_____

_____

Can you think of some type of visual trigger you can use that will remind you to do your new habit? For example, putting your vitamins on the kitchen counter or setting your exercise clothes out the night before?

_____

_____

_____

_____

_____

_____

_____

_____

Are there any habits you want to let go of? What is your plan for changing these habits?

_____

_____

_____

_____

_____

_____

_____

_____

_____

_____

Week 5

"Focus on What You Want, Not on What You Don't Want"

Mother Teresa once declined an invitation to participate in an anti-war rally. She told them that she was not interested in an anti-war rally, but she would be happy to participate in a pro-peace rally.

Why do we spend so much of our time focusing on what we DON'T want, instead of focusing on what we DO want?

It is much harder to lose weight if you tell yourself over and over again how fat you are. It is almost impossible to feel well, if you do nothing but talk about how sick you feel. It is much harder to attract money and experience abundance, if every other word you speak is about "lack" or "not enough."

I have great "parking karma." I always find a great parking spot, because I expect it to be there. One day, however, I had an appointment downtown and the parking lot was very crowded. I mumbled to myself, "I'm never going to be able to find a space at this time of day." And sure enough, I didn't see any open spaces. But then I reminded myself that I had "good parking karma" and when I looked around, I discovered that there was an open space right in front of me. I just hadn't seen it because I didn't expect it to be there. It was like I was blind to what was right in front of me.

The moral of the story is to focus on what you want, not on what you don't want. The things that you want are right there in front of your eyes, you just can't see them until you expect to see them.

Like attracts like. Cheerful people attract other cheerful people. Gloomy people attract other gloomy people. Likewise, if you want more abundance in your life, you have to focus on the abundance you already have. If you want better health, you have to focus on the good health you already enjoy.

This week you are going to consciously focus on the things in your life that you like, the things you wouldn't mind having more of. And you are also going to become aware of the words you use throughout the day that may be focusing your attention on what you don't want, instead of on what you do want.

Remember, that parking space was right there in front of my eyes. **I just didn't see it until I expected to see it.**

Monday

Week 5 - "Focus on What You Want, Not on What You Don't Want"

Monday

What good things do you want to attract today?

_____

_____

What good things came your way today?

_____

_____

_____

Were there times you caught yourself thinking or saying negative things? What about?

_____

_____

_____

How are you going to focus more on the positive than on the negative?

_____

_____

_____

What are you grateful for today?

_____

_____

Tuesday

Week 5 - "Focus on What You Want, Not on What You Don't Want"

Tuesday

What good things do you want to attract today?

_____

_____

What good things came your way today?

_____

_____

_____

Were there times you caught yourself thinking or saying negative things? What about?

_____

_____

_____

How are you going to focus more on the positive than on the negative?

_____

_____

_____

What are you grateful for today?

_____

_____

Wednesday

Week 5 - "Focus on What You Want, Not on What You Don't Want"

Wednesday

What good things do you want to attract today?

_____

_____

What good things came your way today?

_____

_____

_____

Were there times you caught yourself thinking or saying negative things? What about?

_____

_____

_____

How are you going to focus more on the positive than on the negative?

_____

_____

_____

What are you grateful for today?

_____

_____

Thursday

Week 5 - "Focus on What You Want, Not on What You Don't Want"

Thursday

What good things do you want to attract today?

_____

_____

What good things came your way today?

_____

_____

_____

Were there times you caught yourself thinking or saying negative things? What about?

_____

_____

_____

How are you going to focus more on the positive than on the negative?

_____

_____

_____

What are you grateful for today?

_____

_____

Friday

To-Do's

Friday

What good things do you want to attract today?

_____

_____

What good things came your way today?

_____

_____

_____

Were there times you caught yourself thinking or saying negative things? What about?

_____

_____

_____

How are you going to focus more on the positive than on the negative?

_____

_____

_____

What are you grateful for today?

_____

_____

Saturday & Sunday

What did you discover about yourself this week?

_____

_____

_____

_____

_____

Do you say kind things about your body when you look in the mirror?

_____

_____

_____

_____

_____

How do you talk about money? Do you complain about money a lot? Or do you use positive words, like "plenty" or "more than enough?"

_____

_____

_____

_____

_____

How often do you fall into "victim mode," complaining how this person or that person "done you wrong?"

_____

_____

_____

_____

Is there an area of your life where you consistently focus on the positive and use positive words? Why do you think you feel so good about this area of your life?

_____

_____

_____

_____

How did you experience the "law of attraction" this week? Did you find that you attracted more good things to your life when you were focused on the good things you already have?

_____

_____

_____

_____

Week 6

"The Universe is Just Throwing Money at Me!"

If you are like most people, you probably have very mixed feelings when it comes to money. Our society villainizes people with money. Notice the words that are used in the newspapers and listen to the way people speak. People with money are portrayed as greedy and not to be trusted. Whereas the poor and suffering are often portrayed as selfless heroes.

Many people also consciously or subconsciously think of money as "the root of all evil" or as "filthy lucre," and fear that they can't be a good person and have money too. Another fear is that if we have lots of money our friends won't like us anymore. Or that they will want something from us all of the time.

Yet when we have money in our life, it feels pretty darn good. When extra money comes in, it is usually a joyful experience. It takes the pressure off. Last week, you were encouraged to start noticing the open parking spaces all around you. This week I encourage you to notice all the abundance around you.

Here's a fun game I like to play. Whenever I find a coin on the street or in the couch cushions, I pick the coin up and say, "The universe is just throwing money at me!" I keep all these coins in a container that I label with a note saying: "Abundance is all around me. I just have to notice it."

Give some special thought this week as to what type of "money words" work for you. For example, phrases like "I want to be rich" or "I want to be a millionaire" may put you under too much pressure or may feel unrealistic and unattainable. Perhaps a phrase like this would work better for you: "It feels so good to have plenty of money for all the things I want to do."

Abundance comes in many forms -- abundance of health, abundance of beauty, abundance of love. But for this week, we're going to be focusing on monetary abundance. Most people wish they had more money, so this week you are going to train yourself to see the opportunities for money that are already all around you.

Once you start expecting abundance and looking for examples of abundance, you begin to see it everywhere. And you begin to allow more of it into your life.

Monday

To-Do's

Monday

What positive experiences will you have today regarding money?

_____

_____

_____

_____

In what ways did you attract money today?

_____

_____

_____

_____

How did you experience abundance today?

_____

_____

_____

What are you grateful for today?

_____

_____

_____

_____

Tuesday

Tuesday

What positive experiences will you have today regarding money?

_____

_____

_____

_____

In what ways did you attract money today?

_____

_____

_____

_____

How did you experience abundance today?

_____

_____

_____

What are you grateful for today?

_____

_____

_____

_____

Wednesday

Wednesday

What positive experiences will you have today regarding money?

_____

_____

_____

_____

In what ways did you attract money today?

_____

_____

_____

_____

How did you experience abundance today?

_____

_____

_____

What are you grateful for today?

_____

_____

_____

_____

Thursday

Thursday

What positive experiences will you have today regarding money?

_____
_____
_____
_____

In what ways did you attract money today?

_____
_____
_____
_____

How did you experience abundance today?

_____
_____
_____

What are you grateful for today?

_____
_____
_____
_____

Friday

To-Do's

Friday

What positive experiences will you have today regarding money?

_____

_____

_____

_____

In what ways did you attract money today?

_____

_____

_____

_____

How did you experience abundance today?

_____

_____

_____

What are you grateful for today?

_____

_____

_____

_____

Saturday & Sunday

Did you have a chance this week to pay attention to the way people speak about money? What did you notice?

_____

_____

_____

_____

_____

_____

_____

_____

_____

_____

Do you feel differently now about money than you did before? What have you learned? How have you grown?

Are there any changes you want to make in your life, having to do with money?

In what other areas of your life are you experiencing abundance?

Week 7

"Self-Fulfilling Prophecy"

"Law of attraction" and "self-fulfilling prophecy" are very similar. Law of attraction is usually about "things" you want to attract, and self-fulfilling prophecy is usually about the kind of person you want to be.

For the most part, self-fulfilling prophecy is something we do subconsciously. For example, if you think of yourself, either consciously or subconsciously, as a "dumb blond," you will most likely fulfill that expectation of yourself by saying things and acting in ways that others perceive as "dumb."

Self-fulfilling prophecy is a negative or positive prediction you have about yourself that invariably comes true. "I knew that was going to happen." "I knew I wouldn't be able to do that." Let me repeat. Self-fulfilling prophecy is a prediction you make about yourself that comes true.

Many times, the expectations you have for yourself come from the way you were raised. When asked why she hadn't applied to college, my daughter's friend said, "I'm a Taylor. We don't go to college."

Self-fulfilling prophecy is why affirmations work. Affirmations are statements about yourself that you write down and say out loud every day. For example, a friend of mine has a note taped to her mirror that says, "I am beautiful, kind, and I have a great sense of humor."

This week, with the help of the journal prompts, you are going to become aware of both the positive and negative ways you may be using self-fulfilling prophecy. **If you are going to be making predictions about your future, let's make sure they are positive predictions.** What's that saying? Whether you think you are smart or you think you are stupid, you are right.

Monday

To-Do's

Monday

What positive outcomes are you predicting for yourself today?

_____

_____

_____

_____

How did you experience self-fulfilling prophecy today?

_____

_____

_____

_____

Did you catch yourself expecting something negative to happen?
How are you going to change that?

_____

_____

_____

What are you grateful for today?

_____

_____

_____

_____

Tuesday

Tuesday

What positive outcomes are you predicting for yourself today?

_____

_____

_____

_____

How did you experience self-fulfilling prophecy today?

_____

_____

_____

_____

Did you catch yourself expecting something negative to happen?
How are you going to change that?

_____

_____

_____

What are you grateful for today?

_____

_____

_____

_____

Wednesday

Wednesday

What positive outcomes are you predicting for yourself today?

_____

_____

_____

_____

How did you experience self-fulfilling prophecy today?

_____

_____

_____

_____

Did you catch yourself expecting something negative to happen?
How are you going to change that?

_____

_____

_____

What are you grateful for today?

_____

_____

_____

_____

Thursday

To-Do's

Thursday

What positive outcomes are you predicting for yourself today?

How did you experience self-fulfilling prophecy today?

Did you catch yourself expecting something negative to happen?
How are you going to change that?

What are you grateful for today?

Friday

Friday

What positive outcomes are you predicting for yourself today?

How did you experience self-fulfilling prophecy today?

Did you catch yourself expecting something negative to happen?
How are you going to change that?

What are you grateful for today?

Saturday & Sunday

What have you discovered about the types of self-fulfilling prophecies you have for yourself?

_____

_____

_____

_____

_____

_____

_____

_____

_____

What predictions are you making for your future?

_____

_____

_____

_____

_____

_____

Where do you think most of your predictions come from?
From your family, your friends, or from society?

_____

_____

_____

_____

_____

What can you do to make sure you have only positive predictions
about your future?

_____

_____

_____

_____

_____

_____

Week 8

"Act As If..."

I agreed to take a yoga class with a friend of mine, but when I arrived at the class I found myself feeling uncomfortable and self-conscious. So I decided to "act as if" I took yoga all the time and that I knew what to do. The transformation was amazing. I began to move more fluidly. I understood the instructions better. Physically, I was just as un-bendy as I was before I decided to play the "act as if" game, but pretending to myself that I took yoga all the time had me doing the movements with more confidence and a bit more panache.

"Act as if" is a powerful principle and I invite you to give it a try. So many times we let nervousness or insecurity get in our way. But acting as if we are comfortable in the situation becomes a type of self-fulfilling prophecy and we actually do become more comfortable.

Here are some ways you can play the "act as if" game:

Not sure of your skills in the kitchen? Act as if you are a gourmet chef and see what happens. Feeling uncomfortable in a business meeting? Act as if you are the CEO and you know exactly what you are doing. Have to give a speech? Act as if you give speeches all the time. If you are a student, act as if you are an "A" student.

A word of caution, however. This is an internal game you play in your head. You don't actually tell others you are a gourmet chef, a yoga master, or CEO of the company. That would get you a far different result, most likely a padded room.

The goal this week is to identify those moments in your day when you feel uncomfortable or insecure. **Then act as if you know what you are doing and see what happens.** I think you are going to be very happy with the results.

Monday

To-Do's

Week 8 - "Act As If..."

Monday

Today, I am going to act as if. . .

_____

_____

_____

How did "acting as if" make you feel? Did it work for you?

_____

_____

_____

What did you learn from today?

_____

_____

_____

In what areas of your life would it be helpful to "act as if" more often?

_____

_____

_____

What are you grateful for today?

_____

_____

_____

Tuesday

To-Do's

Tuesday

Today, I am going to act as if. . .

_____

_____

_____

How did "acting as if" make you feel? Did it work for you?

_____

_____

_____

What did you learn from today?

_____

_____

_____

In what areas of your life would it be helpful to "act as if" more often?

_____

_____

_____

What are you grateful for today?

_____

_____

_____

Wednesday

Week 8 - "Act As If..."

Wednesday

Today, I am going to act as if. . .

_____

_____

_____

How did "acting as if" make you feel? Did it work for you?

_____

_____

_____

What did you learn from today?

_____

_____

_____

In what areas of your life would it be helpful to "act as if" more often?

_____

_____

_____

What are you grateful for today?

_____

_____

_____

_____

Thursday

Thursday

Today, I am going to act as if. . .

_____

_____

_____

How did "acting as if" make you feel? Did it work for you?

_____

_____

_____

What did you learn from today?

_____

_____

_____

In what areas of your life would it be helpful to "act as if" more often?

_____

_____

_____

What are you grateful for today?

_____

_____

_____

Friday

To-Do's

Week 8 - "Act As If..."

Friday

Today, I am going to act as if. . .

_____

_____

_____

How did "acting as if" make you feel? Did it work for you?

_____

_____

What did you learn from today?

_____

_____

In what areas of your life would it be helpful to "act as if" more often?

_____

_____

What are you grateful for today?

_____

_____

_____

_____

Saturday & Sunday

In what types of situations was the "act as if" game most helpful to you? Was it when you were trying something new? Meeting new people?

_____

_____

_____

_____

_____

_____

_____

_____

_____

_____

_____

One of the reasons "act as if" works so well is that it gets us past a fear of failure. So many times we don't even try something, because we think we might fail at it. If you could do anything, with no possibility of failure and money was not an issue, what would you do?

Looking into the future, do you see some situations where "acting as if" would be helpful to you?

Week 9

"The Power of Visualization"

When Michael Phelps was training for the Olympics, his coach had him visualize different types of races in his head every night before he went to bed. Once, in one of his real races, his goggles fogged up and he was unable to see the lane dividers, the line on the bottom of the pool, or the wall at the end of the pool. But because he had practiced this type of scenario in his head, over and over, he knew exactly what to do and was able to win the race.

Prisoners of War (POW) use visualization too. They will play golf in their head or practice the piano in their head. And when they are released, they find that their golf game and their piano playing has improved. Even though they only practiced it in their head.

This is pretty amazing stuff. The question then is, how can you use visualization to improve your own life?

Do you know what your goals are? Before you turn the page, I want you to write down three goals that you would like to achieve this week.

Goal #1:

_____

_____

_____

Goal #2:

_____

_____

_____

Goal #3:

_____

_____

_____

Now, for the next week, you are going to picture in your mind that you have already achieved these goals. I want you to see as much detail as possible and I want you to feel, in as big as way as possible, how wonderful it is when you achieve each of these goals.

Monday

Monday

What goal or goals are you going to visualize achieving?

_____

_____

_____

How did you feel at the end of the visualization exercise?

_____

_____

_____

Did visualizing what you want, help you in some way today?

_____

_____

_____

What other things do you want to visualize?

_____

_____

_____

What are you grateful for today?

_____

_____

_____

_____

Tuesday

To-Do's

Tuesday

What goal or goals are you going to visualize achieving?

How did you feel at the end of the visualization exercise?

Did visualizing what you want, help you in some way today?

What other things do you want to visualize?

What are you grateful for today?

Wednesday

Wednesday

What goal or goals are you going to visualize achieving?

_____

_____

_____

How did you feel at the end of the visualization exercise?

_____

_____

_____

Did visualizing what you want, help you in some way today?

_____

_____

_____

What other things do you want to visualize?

_____

_____

_____

What are you grateful for today?

_____

_____

_____

_____

Thursday

To-Do's

Thursday

What goal or goals are you going to visualize achieving?

_____

_____

_____

How did you feel at the end of the visualization exercise?

_____

_____

_____

Did visualizing what you want, help you in some way today?

_____

_____

_____

What other things do you want to visualize?

_____

_____

_____

What are you grateful for today?

_____

_____

_____

_____

Friday

To-Do's

Friday

What goal or goals are you going to visualize achieving?

_____

_____

How did you feel at the end of the visualization exercise?

_____

_____

Did visualizing what you want, help you in some way today?

_____

_____

What other things do you want to visualize?

_____

_____

What are you grateful for today?

_____

_____

_____

Saturday & Sunday

Did you find that visualizing your goals made them feel more familiar and therefore more achievable?

_____

_____

_____

_____

_____

_____

_____

_____

_____

_____

Regarding the three goals you wrote down at the beginning of this week, will you be modifying them, as a result of this exercise? If so, how?

Going forward, in what ways will you use visualization to help make your life easier and better?

You've now been using Joy Journal for nine weeks. Have you come up with any other goals you'd like to achieve? Perhaps regarding your health, your finances, your family, or your career? If so, write them here. Writing them down makes them more real, and will help you achieve them.

Week 10

"Set Yourself Up For Success"

"Set yourself up for success" means to do the things, both little and big, that increases your chance of being successful. Getting a college degree, depending on your field, may be a way of setting yourself up for success. Preparing for a business presentation is setting yourself up for success. As is studying for a test.

Setting yourself up for success can also be little things. Like not leaving your purse in the shopping cart, where it could be stolen. Or not leaving toys on the stairs where someone could trip on them.

There are also things we do that are not helpful and may actually be setting us up for failure. Partying the night before a test. Not going to class. Showing up late for work. Waiting until the last minute to get things done. Ruining your reputation by not doing what you say you are going to do. Spending more than you earn. Driving recklessly. Waiting until the gas tank is on fumes before you get gas. Not telling the truth. Having a "victim mentality" where you blame others for what's wrong in your life. Developing bad habits, instead of good habits. Disliking everyone you meet. Cheating on your taxes. Not telling the people who care about you how you really feel. Living the life you think others want you to live, instead of a life that brings you joy. Putting off happiness until another day, then another day, then another day.

This week you are going to look at your life with fresh eyes so that you can identify the things you are doing that are setting you up for failure, and the things you are doing that are setting you up for success.

Be gentle with yourself when you do these exercises. No one intentionally sets themself up for failure. Usually, it's just because we are wrapped up in the moment or the busy-ness of life, and we don't realize that our short term actions will have negative long term consequences.

In Week Five, we talked about the importance of focusing on what you want, not on what you don't want. So we are going to focus on "setting yourself up for failure" just for a bit. Just long enough for you to become aware of anything you are doing that you might want to change. **Then we are going to go right back to finding easy and sustainable things you can do to set yourself up for success.**

Monday

To-Do's

Monday

How are you going to set yourself up for success today?

How did that turn out for you? Did it work?

What other things can you do to help yourself succeed?

Did you do anything today that you think might set yourself up for "failure?" Do you want to change that, and if so, how?

What are you grateful for today?

Tuesday

Tuesday

How are you going to set yourself up for success today?

_____

_____

_____

How did that turn out for you? Did it work?

_____

_____

_____

What other things can you do to help yourself succeed?

_____

_____

_____

Did you do anything today that you think might set yourself up for "failure?" Do you want to change that, and if so, how?

_____

_____

_____

What are you grateful for today?

_____

_____

_____

Wednesday

Wednesday

How are you going to set yourself up for success today?

How did that turn out for you? Did it work?

What other things can you do to help yourself succeed?

Did you do anything today that you think might set yourself up for "failure?" Do you want to change that, and if so, how?

What are you grateful for today?

Thursday

To-Do's

Thursday

How are you going to set yourself up for success today?

_____

_____

_____

How did that turn out for you? Did it work?

_____

_____

_____

What other things can you do to help yourself succeed?

_____

_____

_____

Did you do anything today that you think might set yourself up for "failure?" Do you want to change that, and if so, how?

_____

_____

_____

What are you grateful for today?

_____

_____

_____

Friday

Friday

How are you going to set yourself up for success today?

_____

_____

_____

How did that turn out for you? Did it work?

_____

_____

_____

What other things can you do to help yourself succeed?

_____

_____

_____

Did you do anything today that you think might set yourself up for "failure?" Do you want to change that, and if so, how?

_____

_____

_____

What are you grateful for today?

_____

_____

_____

Saturday & Sunday

What did you learn about yourself this week?

_____

_____

_____

_____

_____

_____

_____

_____

_____

_____

Are there any changes you want to make with the way you do things?

_____

_____

_____

_____

_____

_____

_____

_____

_____

What are you doing that you want to keep on doing?

_____

_____

_____

_____

_____

_____

_____

_____

_____

Week 11

"What Are You Excited About?"

Helen Keller once wrote, "Life is a daring adventure or nothing at all."

Is your life an adventure?

_____

_____

Do you like what you are doing?

_____

_____

Do you like where you are heading?

_____

_____

It's important to pay attention to the exciting parts of your life. The things that are fun. Those special moments that fuel your day and make you want to get out of bed in the morning.

Everyone has a different idea of what is exciting. For one person it is writing a book. For someone else it is decorating a room. For someone else it is waiting for their kids to get home from school. One of the quickest ways to feel excited about your day is to switch from "should-do" mode into "want-to" mode.

What do you WANT to do this week? What sounds fun? What would feel light and joyous? Is there anything in particular that you are looking forward to? What makes you happy?

_____

_____

_____

_____

_____

This week is going to be a great week. This week you get to focus on the things that are the most exciting to you.

Monday

Monday

What are you looking forward to today?

_____

_____

_____

Is this something unique to today? Or is this something that you always enjoy?

_____

_____

_____

What other types of things do you get excited about?

_____

_____

_____

How can you add more of these exciting things to your life more often?

_____

_____

_____

What are you grateful for today?

_____

_____

_____

_____

Tuesday

To-Do's

Tuesday

What are you looking forward to today?

_____

_____

_____

Is this something unique to today? Or is this something that you always enjoy?

_____

_____

_____

What other types of things do you get excited about?

_____

_____

_____

How can you add more of these exciting things to your life more often?

_____

_____

_____

What are you grateful for today?

_____

_____

_____

_____

Wednesday

Wednesday

What are you looking forward to today?

_____

_____

_____

Is this something unique to today? Or is this something that you always enjoy?

_____

_____

_____

What other types of things do you get excited about?

_____

_____

_____

How can you add more of these exciting things to your life more often?

_____

_____

_____

What are you grateful for today?

_____

_____

_____

_____

Thursday

Thursday

What are you looking forward to today?

_____

_____

_____

Is this something unique to today? Or is this something that you always enjoy?

_____

_____

_____

What other types of things do you get excited about?

_____

_____

_____

How can you add more of these exciting things to your life more often?

_____

_____

_____

What are you grateful for today?

_____

_____

_____

Friday

To-Do's

Friday

What are you looking forward to today?

_____

_____

_____

Is this something unique to today? Or is this something that you always enjoy?

_____

_____

_____

What other types of things do you get excited about?

_____

_____

_____

How can you add more of these exciting things to your life more often?

_____

_____

_____

What are you grateful for today?

_____

_____

_____

Saturday & Sunday

How do you feel this weekend? Do you feel lighter and happier?
Less burdened?

_____

_____

_____

_____

_____

_____

_____

_____

_____

Did you notice that you get more done when you are happy and enthusiastic about what you are doing?

_____

_____

_____

_____

Did you learn a trick or technique this week that you can use in the future to get you out of a "nose-to-the-grindstone" mode and back into joy mode?

_____

_____

_____

_____

What are the types of things that make you happy?

_____

_____

_____

_____

How can you feel happy and enthusiastic and joyful more of the time?

_____

_____

_____

_____

Week 12

"Taking Care of Yourself"

Rechargeable

I will not be a disposable battery,
One used up and quickly tossed.

I will recharge.
I'll freshen my head.

I'll plug myself in,
And recharge in bed.

There's no doubt about it. Fatigue is a joy-killer. It's awfully hard to feel happy and joyful when you are tired.

My guess is that you already know what you need to do in order to recharge your batteries. You probably just don't do it often enough.

One of the biggest reasons people don't rest and recharge is because they "don't have the time." But once you are rested, you get so much more done and things flow so much more easily. Plus, what's the point of getting a lot done, if you don't enjoy yourself in the process? What's the point, if you are not enjoying your life?

So this week, and every week, make a promise to pace yourself. Life is a marathon, not a sprint. Recharge along the way and you will enjoy your life so much more. **It isn't selfish to take care of yourself. It's just common sense. You can serve others better when you are in good shape.**

Monday

To-Do's

Monday

How are you going to take care of yourself today?

_____

_____

_____

_____

Were you able to take care of yourself the way you had planned?
Why or why not?

_____

_____

_____

What changes do you need to make, if any, for tomorrow?

_____

_____

_____

What are you grateful for today?

_____

_____

_____

_____

Tuesday

To-Do's

Tuesday

How are you going to take care of yourself today?

_____

_____

_____

_____

Were you able to take care of yourself the way you had planned?
Why or why not?

_____

_____

_____

What changes do you need to make, if any, for tomorrow?

_____

_____

_____

What are you grateful for today?

_____

_____

_____

_____

Wednesday

Wednesday

How are you going to take care of yourself today?

_____

_____

_____

_____

Were you able to take care of yourself the way you had planned?
Why or why not?

_____

_____

_____

What changes do you need to make, if any, for tomorrow?

_____

_____

_____

_____

What are you grateful for today?

_____

_____

_____

_____

Thursday

To-Do's

Thursday

How are you going to take care of yourself today?

_____

_____

_____

_____

Were you able to take care of yourself the way you had planned?
Why or why not?

_____

_____

_____

What changes do you need to make, if any, for tomorrow?

_____

_____

_____

What are you grateful for today?

_____

_____

_____

_____

Friday

To-Do's

Friday

How are you going to take care of yourself today?

_____

_____

_____

_____

Were you able to take care of yourself the way you had planned?
Why or why not?

_____

_____

_____

What changes do you need to make, if any, for tomorrow?

_____

_____

_____

_____

What are you grateful for today?

_____

_____

_____

_____

Saturday & Sunday

I hope that Joy Journal has helped make your life a little bit better. It's so easy to get wrapped up in the busy-ness of life that we forget to stop and smell the roses. We forget to notice how good our life already is. This may be the end of this journal, but it is just the beginning for you. May your days always be joyful, fun, productive, and filled with delightful surprises.

What is the most important thing you learned from Joy Journal?

Which of the concepts was the most helpful to you?

Will it be helpful to you to continue writing a daily journal? If so, what's your plan?

Did you find that planning in advance to have a good day, stabilized your moods and made your days better?

Author's Note

I originally created Joy Journal because I needed something to even out my moods and help me see the brighter side of things. Writing in my "Joy Journal," as I came to call it, quickly became one of my favorite things to do.

In the mornings, I sat out on my backyard deck with a cup of chai tea and planned out all the ways my day would be wonderful. Soon, I realized that all the pages were filled and I was preparing to make another journal for myself. My sister and my friends saw my new journal and asked me to print them a copy too.

This made me wonder if others might want the same sort of process for themselves. The question opened a new door for me in the way that I think. Now, as I sit out on my deck, sipping my morning chai, I plan out new Joy Journals -- one for weight and body image, one for financial abundance -- as well as special journals for moms, teens and grandmothers.

I truly hope Joy Journal helps you as much as it has helped me. There is something magical about deciding ahead of time that your days are going to be wonderful. Somehow it tunes you in to all the beautiful and enjoyable possibilities that are already all around you.

Rebecca Kochenderfer

79587943R00104

Made in the USA
Middletown, DE
11 July 2018